I0200719

# Star Traveling©

By

Richard Theodor Kusiolek



ISBN-10: 0615650481

IBSN-13: 978-0615650487

Dedication

I was inspired to complete this collection of poems by children of my family, who were born angels reaching out with their spirit of love, joy, and heavenly balance. - Jim Warwick, Linda Warwick, Ken Warwick, Mark Warwick, Tracy Gutierrez and Denise Novak- Melissa Rose Kusiolek, Christopher Robert Kusiolek, Mariana Varzia Kusiolek,.

Star Traveling is a collection of free-verse American poems spanning the authors years of poetic insights. Since at a very young age, when given the opportunity to spend his summers in Hamlet Indiana, he began to star travel. He would lie on the grass surrounding his grandparent's farmhouse and stare into the vast night skies. He watched the brilliance of those stars in the high heavens and dreamed of star traveling. Those moments were the beginning of a desire to write short poems to express the wonder of life and always travel to the stars-islands of light. Star traveling spanned the majestic starlit skies over Mount Fuji-Japan, Daming Palace-Xi'an China, Lake Baikal-Russia, Atherton Forest-Australia, Tarapoto-Peru, Cozumel-Mexico, Yosemite National Park-California, and The Grand Canyon-Arizona.

(3-11-1962)

## The Goddess Muza

Gaze upon the woman

A goddess they say

To the pinnacle

Of mighty Mount Olympus

She strives

Zeus heralds her coming

Oh Goddess

Immortality onward

Rest upon

Soft dew gathered clouds

He beckons

For this is thy nectar

Fade away

Oh Goddess

So fair but a dream

I had hoped for

Mine eyes destroyeth

No soul

Love ruleth me

Immortal man

Never be

Fade away

**(4-5-1962)**

## Ode to Womanly Perfection

Oh!  Fools are we, Can you not be but a myth to me?

Why do I go on so to feel but only to die?

Truth but dies on this vine

Suffering slowly destroy my immortal soul

Forget this, for an island such as yours, Can never be bridged

The waves but sweep it aside

To fight but not to gain I but push onward to new shores

I shall stand but alone for the grave is my only home

The footprints in the sand shall disappear

Slowly the crumbling sand takes away all trace

I bid you farewell for I have played the game

Not even a thorn-burdened crown shall be mine

I walk away in disgrace

Oh callous and wicked fops they be

Who swallow pride to rush upon the sea

To clutch only droplets

Of diluted sleep

**(3-29-1963)**

**Jane and Joby**

With great joy upon my laden soul
A breath of acknowledgement
Suffering though I be
Two golden silver stallions snorted by
Gave to me that wondrous ride
Past eternity

Simple man is I
Genius never be
Mind not heart
Suffer for thee

My soul darkened
My mind firm
Heart burning so

As I flew past the valley
The trees bent as to speak
Fool he be
Time is eternal
Why suffer thee?

**(4-5-1963)**

**Fuchu, Japan**

Oh! World of cries
Thou art but hopeless lies
I sit here to seek the ring
I hear only the heart
Subconscious sting
Locked within

The bell of all
Why, or for what
Straw of life that withers
Shine above
The soul be many
The flesh but few
Oh, ye worry not
For laurels not to be mine
I cry only within
Laden with sin

The spirit locked
Demands to be free
Let me out, Now, Oh silly fool
Spin again
This is my last!

## (6-13-1963)

## Fujisawa, Japan

The bird's wings of auburn black

Dropped from a shattered stem

And came tumbling down upon

Blinding sea and sand

Floundered on this bird

With wings of auburn black

Your course straight

Regardless of attack

Come back

## (8-14-1963)

## Blue Sparkles

Recede across the blue plain

Sparkle with life

Every act be so mundane

I strive to be sane

Anchor thrown between the waves

Beyond be only caves

Look above and not a tear

For destruction be only fear

## (12-18-1963)

## Kyoto Japan

The warmth was too seductive.

I captured a nap under the sun and there

I heard the soft warbling of sparrows.

The breeze stroked passed my nostrils.

I eagerly devoured its sweetness.

## (12-19-1963)

## Muza Kemina

The dormant sea upon a river’s edge

Lilies lay both black and white

You came to me murmuring

Love is a dark sleep

## (8-19-1963)

## My JoAnn

JoAnn young girl for an old man

I first saw you jumping across park puddles

Sweet young JoAnn why for an old man

Smiling so deceivingly caught the heart of an old man

Trailing small lips for an old man

Up turned breast, Soft thighs

Love ever flowing ever gushing

For the grasp of an old man

(4-5-1977)

## Janice's Escape

Whispering glen

Encased Moon

Mindless

Wavering reflections

Upon the midnight sky

Slow trickling

Tear Upon

Roughened face

Crying spirit

Saddened by

Hollowed voices upon

The shadowed screens

Standing upon

Palm desert

Sprinkled terraces of thoughts

Blackened fingers

Grasping for life

Sounds of slipping away

Lay nothingness

But a quivering breath

**(4-15-1977)**

**Alice Sicilian**

Noon drops of haze

Purple sequenced cries

Blackened wells of despair

Soft flap of giant birds

You entered my domain

Twisted and disorderly

Poking your upside down smile

Into my bright sunshine

Your lips uttered

Love me

Time was never a soft companion

Words meant nothing

Your bright lucid moments

You promised your heart

Swinging Lucite doors to your

Vast plains of possibilities

When I stopped and said no

Your dark blinking eyes conveyed

Love me

**(12-12-1978)**

**Ft. Madison, Iowa**

Can life be nothing less?

Than sequences of struggles

Renewing and redirecting

Our selves towards some

Super governing

Objective for the betterment

Of universal organ transplants

**(7-30-1980)**

**Redwood City, California**

We lay within visions

Sugared and warm

And unique

Each in brown covers

Like a cocoon

All willing to explode

Into flowing white foam

Some without strength

Reaching for blissful

Kisses of forgetfulness

**(1-27-1982)**

## Searching for Self

Vacuous stares, hallowed chambers

Distant glimmers, oozing, and blending

Into pools of despair and emptiness

Dried membranes, Walking sounds

Vibrating against three pillars

Hope, Despair, Renewal

Rejected memories, forgotten thoughts

Societal projections, Self-propelled glares of reality

Light induced profiles, Clustered sounds of iced pyramids

Sterilized and neutralized images, Hopes distilled into

Fortune studded canisters, Made-up clowns

Playing business and order

Grasping only identifiable hands

Clouds open and close

Wind and ancestral dust

Blows in nostrils and lungs

Are we dreaming?

We are agents of liberalization

Dashing between many

Lights of reality

**(2-11-1982)**

## Sarah

Nickel flavored lips

White entrenched hips

Red stained smiles

Windmills

Jaws swaying

Pacific Ocean dying

**(4-18-1982)**

## Who

The sound of zephyr smiles

Upon neon flashes

Idealistic thoughts

As distant melodies of surf

Quest and whispers

I exist for you

**(6-14-1982)**

## Phoenix Arizona

Solitary traps

Encapsulated raps

Distant swirls of eras

Sounds of panting regurgitations

Love and revelations

Messages standard

Listeners with cacophonic disparity

Phoenix land of dead birds

Searching for rebirthing sentinels

Green and yellowed

Pocketed and scheduled

Coined and urbane

**(7-3-1982)**

## Glow

In the shining light

Your eyes

Seeing distant skies

Glowing whimsical melodies

Aphrodisiac watermelons

**(8-1-1982)**

## Alone

Hands stretching

Towards shadows

Faces receding

Upon gallows

Voices grasping

Nights elapsing

Light turned to stone

Inner projections

Again

Alone

**(11-6-1982)**

## Receding Star

A receding star, a chasm of sight

The beacons in the night, your eyes aglow in the light

Touching grasping hands, sounding the drum pulses of life

Like a flower opening, your parting lips whispered

Hold me and keep me glowing

I saw your light mantel, Bright was the night

You whispered, Take my hand

Together let us push away

Fear blankets of delight

**(12-1-1982)**

## Remembering

Do you remember me?

When my life was not so free

Do you remember me?

Shadowed by the light

Closing away sight

When my life was not so free

Do you remember me?

Seeking only your hand

Making a grand stand

When my life was not so free

Do you remember me?

Whispering are you the one

Who will set me free?

When my life was not so free

Do you remember me?

(2-20-1984)

## Women

Pregnant calling voice
A child shall become
A golden vessel
For the Lord
The giver of our light
And our shadows

Perhaps afraid
Looking before us
And touching our hands
On the winds of our
Present need for despair
Or to hold our hands
On the soft womb of life

(6-12-1984)

## Sign Post

Love God
Fight for Justice
Fight for Honor
Believe in the Power
Be not afraid of the methods

**(6-26-1984)**

## Youth

When the time has gone
Remember the days of illusion
Sand, light, and confusion

**(8-1-1984)**

## Palo Alto Love Dreams

Drifting flow, under the rapid essence
Questing, running, then reaching
Blue voids in a sunlit morning
Cloud shrouded haze
Myths upon the mind

Did you ever exist?
Was it my own need
To touch and hold you?
I remember
When you just smiled, did you think
That I did not notice?
A Moment
Seeking, caressing, plunging, tearing into
Sweat beds of love

**(3-15-1985)**

## Ivy Lane

The Great Sea has sent me adrift

It moves me

As the weed in a Great River

Earth and the Great Power

Moves me

Has carried me away

And moves my inward

Being with Joy

**(1-23-1987)**

## Prism Glowing

Love is an ocean

Constant Motion

Turning into hardened bubbles

Crushing rock to sand

Sand to earth

Earth to growth

Growth to Man

Man to God

**(2-27-1987)**

## Napkin Thoughts

Fear sown

Dreams of terror

Summer sky unraveling

Emeralds held into the light

Stolen from dusty mines

Shadows with voices

The moon is blue

Reality untrue

Light reflecting

God

**(3-16-1987)**

## Miramar Warm Afternoon

Melodic Sounds, Vibrations

Silence of wind-blown flowers

Leaves rolling, Miramar Beach receding

Crystalized waves reflecting, Pools of life beyond sight

Inner locking memories, Institutionalized agents

Revenue sharks, unionized predators

Hallow sounding politicians, Judges old and senile

Coughing, gasping verdicts, Money edicts

Impossible payments, spiraling breath of despair

Towards Stygian shores

**(4-4-1987)**

## Walnut Creek Tilton

Wind and forest

Echoing silently

Waves on the shore breathing

Come unto me

My love

Breathe the Wind

Smelling the early dew

Come unto me

My love

Silent flowers

Swaying

Warmed by Ocean

Along the sand cliffs

Foam clouds

Racing

Eyes viewing

Smashing love sounds

Come unto me

My love

**(4-7-1987)**

**Sun Moon**

The Sun Shines

Whether you live or die

Like Magic

When pushed down

It comes up

For nothing can stop change

Nothing can hold back

The light of love

I yearn only for your smile

For only the smell of your skin

Close to my lips

For only the feel of your

Warm hardened breast

Brings back the Spirit

The Mind and the Light

Of tomorrow

## (6-25-1987)

## Hope

Hope is the thing with feathers

That perches within the soul

And sings the tune without words

And never stops at all

## (6-30-1987) Half Moon Bay

## Debra Moon Bay

Dulcimer Wings

Gliding purple upon the green shoots

Ocean movements, glowing silently

Brown spirits gliding

Diving for energy

Two feathered messengers

Winged following

Laughing breeze

Rolling white, Atmospheric

Elongated rafts, drifting

Dawning movements

Reaching mechanized

Fog shrouded silence

**(8-9-1987)**

**High above Stinson**

Winds whistling across

Rolling highlands of the Dipsea

Shafts of wild wheat bending

Silent hawks gliding free

Calling me

Ocean’s mantel

White foamy waves

Grey ice caps elevated

Rolling mountaintops

Chills ripple across

Skeleton bones

Whistling

Branches extended

Grabbing

Fog cloud droplets

Hawks shrieking

Death swift arriving

Winds sprays chancing

Warm embraces dancing

(7-30-1988)

## Midnight My Dark Beauty

Midnight my sweet dark beauty
You always come to me
With your cares of crying
Some days, I begin to believe
That you only came
To spend just moments
Of friendship time

You never criticize
Then when you are ready
To have me
You sit by my door
Glancing at me
Thanks for being
My only friend
Goodnight
My sweet Midnight

## (2-20-1989)

## Andean Encampment

Snow Flakes upon battlefields

Lifting sound of marching soldiers

Pressing ground of memories

Sounds of powder exploding

Bodies neutralizing

Hell-like voices crying

Sounding melodies

Thundering snowcaps

Pushing masses

Distant fearful voices

Echoes of memories

Love me

My hazel Blue

## (2-25-1989)

## Solitary Thoughts

Time moving, Doors slowly closing

Echoes of farewell, judicial necessities

Crystalized images, Cloudless memories

Wishing thoughts, Solitary agony

Swinging bodies hanging, Blood spattering

Carpets of green

(2-17-1990)

**Redwood City Park- MR Angel**

Oh darkened cloak of fear

That leaves its outreached shadow

Upon my brightest thoughts

Cast away and move to another polarity

Your shocks are painful

Your steps upon my path

Heavy with fear

Your coughing sounds

Of life shattered

The stillness of my evening warmth

Look me not

Your winds of discord

Reach out into the dark voids

Upon the fear laden entrapments

Of manmade laws and Judas's silver

Be still winds

Upon the reach of child born

Soft and shameless

Cast upon the darkened forest

County graft and patronage

Bright Light

Bright house of power

View thy source

Cast us far away

**(3-9-1990)**

**Amby**

Darkened halls, Cavernous whispers
Memories erased
Love and joy replaced
Small hands, Beach castle sands
Prying eye, keeping lies
Goodbye

**(4-18-1990) - *Capitola***

**Melissa Rose Six**

Freeing up the darkness
Beyond fairness, Glad Moments
Turning Sad, Dark Grasping Hands
God's Plans, Distant plains of ice
Turning stones, Darkened skies
Wind Spawned fantasies
Sharpened glass
Stylized flowers
Sea driven Waves
Child of Light
Reflected might
When I held you
Then brilliance
Star light

(4-29-1990)

## Moon Baby

The rain sheeted with gray
Brought me memories of play
Rolling green hills
By the Moon Bay

Whispering voices
Stay
Hoping hands pleading
Make this the day
Reflecting upon Highway One
Upon the window panes

Do you know of me?
Hands upon your ears and eyes
Are you listening to lies?
Do you hear my internal cries?

Dark rolling clouds
Engulfing waves
Shattering sounds of beach sands
Heralding running fever
Child lost
Cold air
Then a breathless quiver

**(7-24-1990)**

## Letter for MRose

As I lived in the illusion of my past

So shall you

Live in the illusion of my memory

As you feel the wind on your cheeks

I shall be with you

As you reach out to understanding

I will grasp your hand

You are now free

Begin your journey

As I so began

Mine

Within the soul of God's

**(3-7-1991)**

## The Romantic

Did I ever tell you that I love you?

Now when I am without you, I feel that I love you

Haunted by you, I longed for you

To share all the sweet moments

Now that I am without you

I only love what I cannot have

Is it not lonely when you have no one?

To share the secrets with

If we stayed, who betrayed our love?

**(3-8-1991)**

## Huntington Beach

I just wanted to stop thinking

To concentrate on

Sun, warm beaches, cool ocean breezes

Opaque ocean reflections

Offshore oilrigs

Eight black suited surfers

Waiting for the wave

That would take them away

**(4-4-1991)**

## Ocean Pain

Cathedral Skies

Lifting Lies

The silence of cries

Reaching out

It all dies

## (4-11-1991)

## "Lord Jim" by Joseph Conrad

*(Reading under a Plum Tree Watsonville CA.)*

What makes pain?

Silence in strength

Pain is man's strength and it is relative

To his imagination

The more imagination

The more pain

Never test a man by your own weakness

No man is a stranger to fear

Fear is a perfect tool for persuasion

What do you fear most? What do you prize most?

What fear could turn the man?

To desert his own goals and principles

## (5-1-1991)

## Lives

What lived once -

Lives forever

**(5-3-1991)**

## Releasing

Letting go

Self-bondage glow

High self-flow

No need to Control

**(5-24-1991)**

## Optional

Leaving you

Was the hardest

Thing for me

I needed to leave

To find stability

And to rebuild my life

**(8-23-1991)**

## Palo Alto Court Room

Historical Garbage

Idealized Baggage

Falling Light, Darkening Might

Sword Drawn, Challenging Scorn

Dripping Eyes, Peace Forlorn

Judicial Scorn

Pure American Corn

**(12-20-1991)**

## Unification

Two strangers looking

Distant and apprehensive

Three years in Silicon Valley prisons

Reaching out, you grabbed my hand

Quickly you smiled

Then we walked onto the land

Of stuffed animals and puppy dogs

We opened the house- they then all fell out

Mickey, Goofy, Bat woman

Spiderman, Ducky, Froggy, and Chickey

Family friends all

Your skin was soft white

Your eyes bright and sensitive

Your spirit courageous and fearless

Radiant with trust and love

Oh, magical child

Must I continue to file

Litigant power

Family tower

Wicked lawyers

Is it time to call?

Diane Sawyer

**(1-4-1992)**

## The American Lawyer

Suffering has no power
No real value of its own
Value out of suffering
Creates only
Profitable Memorials
Of societal death camps

**(1-16-1992)**

## SF Arboretum

Streaming Winds
Engulfing Flames
Harking refrains
Birds alighting
Showered waterfalls
Light warming sun
Soft soaked lips
Punctuated warming
Pulsating tongue flips
Sketch padding
Fingertips
Redwood bench
Decaying stench

**(3-25-1992)**

## Speculation

That chance to heal and be free

I have earned that right

Fifty-two years is a longtime

To work out any curse

A child knows

But gets tired of knowing

**(6-28-1992)**

## Palo Alto Leaves

Whirlwind of shifting leaves

Palo Alto Street Faire remains

Sun-glazed faces and wind embraces

Bubbling ground movements

Sheltering trees swing

Granite-like gazes

Projected upon mirrored canvases

Cloudy images expanding light

Child sweet memory

No longer

A need to fight

**(8-15-1992)**

## Stillness

The stillness of the mind
Brings me closer to now
The beauty and joy of the present
No threats existed
Perfection revealed
Light comes and reflected
Sounds and joys of stillness
What greater joy
Looking out from within

**(8-16-1992)**

## Renewal

The autumn leaves turn
Clouds come
Shore breezes
Body Reaching
Healing

**(11-27-1992)**

## Sheila

Every being is worth receiving, every moment is worth believing

Distant barriers originating, Hallowed valleys, Blackened and retreating

Holding hands in cameo's frame, Lips moving slowly without refrain

Nipples red shaped into fullness, Rounded hips pulsating onto mounded loams of pubic

Spreading layers of soft reddened coves, Kissing entrances of flowing liquidized raves

Sliding up and inward, breathing softly kin ward

Brightened reflected moments upon

Satin lined thighs, separating, and flying

Reaching windward cries, moving towards cascades

Foamy eruptions, fearless breathing, downward trusting

Joyful laughter angered not, past journeys selected without lot

Sliding finger red-eyed finger, Hardened bush-eyed stinger

Rounded toe, sleeping doe, licking moving curled rows

Sliding hand touching calf, grabbing and grasping half

Slow stillness water

Black birds, circling pelicans

Engines revving, Green ocean stillness

White light smiling

Come awhile

**(11-28-1992)**

## Wind

A Change

A metamorphic renewal

Centered woman

Deadly spear

Induced fear

Big and small minds

Numbing senses

Child's light

Shadowing

Spirit

**(12-4-1992)**

## Mountain View Sanctuary

Mind ripples

Likened

Thunderous clay Mountain

Pushing down hope

Stirring dust of despair

Not caring

Mechanical extension

Hopeless believer

Illegal Mexican deceiver

**(3-28-1993)**

## Returning

Cascading sounds over the edge of Muir

Your hair glowed in moments of fear

Pushing back the branches of myself

Heard your song of the Kukabird

Melodic entrenchments

Past trails journeyed far

Wide-eyed and caught in fear

You were far, but never near

Listening only of my thoughts for you

Distant crows calling out

Jays snapping

Circling hawks searching

Arrows pointing

Stepelveidt left, Ben and Bootjack right

Did you really exist?

Were you only living in my dreams?

Gone

The past voices on the Dipsea

**(4-22-1993)**

## M. Rose and I

Like Canyons beyond my mind

Steep graded crevasses, of charred memories

Dreams shattered, Grasping hands

Reaching fog shrouded, Images of what

Could have been, Sand or dry sorted lands

Valley entrances beyond, encased with sounds

Of peacefulness, Feathered Rivers meandering

Blue azures, Brilliance, Reflected dynasties

Of snow-capped mounds, Nested eagles searching horizons

Darkened gloves of, Stewart judgeship jackals

Sniffing air for golden coins, Baugh eyed court appointees

Black robed messengers, of punishment and pain

Down Valley towards, Rocky green sanctuaries

Drum beats of pestilence, Fires leading, Mouths deceiving

Steaming pools of light, laughing voices

Clasping hands, embracing bodies

Children playing, Embraces Swaying

Green meadows of wild grass

Beds of softness, Flowers swaying

Warm sunlight, driven winds

Parchment of sins

**(6-5-1993)**

## Embracing

As I lay watching

Morning starlight

Glistening so bright

Engulfed in your arms

I dreamed of faraway charms

Happiness moment

Holding you close waiting

Golden Sun radiating

Eyes duplicating

Kiss activating

**(9-11-1993)**

## Becky and Craig

Neutrality leads to reality

Reality leads to God

God is the moment that you both hold

Your heart, mind, and body together

The moments

But particles

Of light

Racing molecules

Bombarding

Your joyous moments

God given

Both partaking

**(1-24-1996)**

## There Comes a Time

There comes a time
When we have to say goodbye
Gentle child who I held, but fleeting moments ago
Little feet and charms, happy dancing angel in arms
Believing, struggling, why should you be in harms?

Tick Tock, We raced up the clock
40 hours given, father driven
Stockaded into St. James prison

Child caught in the silicon drift
Billowing brown powder around your wings
Soft tender and white innocence
Heavy with County Court irreverence
Fallen in smog and soot
See how much federalized loot

Clinton’s White House Ravens
Black robed Feminized Jurist
Fingered into oblivion
Child in the silicon
Angel without wings
Please try to sing

**(9-6-1999)**

## Never

So many tides between my thoughts
Reflections that drift me back
Shores of my true undertakings

Meet the process of the present
Struggling away from the dreadful
Feminism stares

Flat bottomed asses with galvanized
Braids of blonde and clothing of purple
Passing generational bridges
Muscled female executioners

New generations
Hardened buttocks
Bisexual, Political gender segments
Spiritless humanoids
Asian lovers
Value-driven holdouts
Slanted stares
Trashing waves
New listening post
Old memory stretches
Upon a canvas
Tibetan sand signs
Goodbye, make believe
Capitola beach dreams

(9-9-1996)

## Silicon Valley Delirium

The delirium of Pain
Will make you insane
Grant you gain
Storms mean a strong sail
New destination, be not afraid
Set the course
Grab the map
Look yonder, Dreams
Warm breezes ahead, Swaying melodies
New friends and lovers

(10-10-1999)

## Dragonfly

Golden dragonfly on a reed
Attacked by a Yellow Jacket
Returning and sunbathing
By the sea
On a sun mist day
Capitola Bay

**(11-9-1999)**

**June River Flowing**

The forest pays tribute to the sun
Birds sing of its glory
Trees reach their limbs skyward
In praise

Good, brown, and warm Earth
Contented smile
Deep in the heart of the day
The Sun and blue heaven itself
Bends to us
Knowing the unreachable

It is a golden world we share
Still waters brushed with gold
They shimmer and gleam
When the wind passes by
The dark places
Of our hearts are made light
The hidden wonders revealed
Mysteries solved
We loved

(1-12-2002)

## Angel in the Wind

Sea smashes

Upon the shores of Brisbane Bay

Beginnings and endings

Where my dreams lay

Wanting to watch

You ran into my arms one more time

Danaher, Stewart, Fogel, Tondreau

Black Jackals dragged you away

Made you die and there you lay

Broken with spine and no longer fine

Waves rushing again

Forgetting watery anger bubbles

Trying not to bend

Progressivism Agenda

Palo Alto had to send

Pacific Gods of rain and wind

Receding back to thoughts of Lynne

Hearing the sounds

Without a fault

No problem Daddy

I am an angel and flying away

Is my default

**(10-21-2003)**

**Xian China**

Upon the Rivers
Scarlet running waters
Orange Brilliance
The sky mist like
Statues crying out
"Launch Forward
Count Down"

Economy class
Filtering lines
Cruel penetrating stares
Centuries walking, Red line
Downcast rhythms
Messenger
Liberator
Mao Zedong

You gave no rain or Sun
Caught upon the mesa of Central China
Darkened by the pulsating shadows
Of past sand-filled drum beats
670 kilometers from your
Close loving embrace
Warm red light beams
Xian, my sword, and shield

**(12-28-2003)**

## Palo Alto Dancing

We are all dancing in Ivy

The wicked die so near

Their children float into seas of fear

Purposeless except in the minds

Mafia studded nail baseball bats

Creators of LGBT society lions

With steel revolving within oily vats

Wind whistling magnolia branches

Six bells sounded after dawn

Twelve victims' red on the lawn

**(11-8-2004)**

## A Day of Dragons

Red Dragons Fly, Opening Sky, Light Blushing

Upon the Hills of Hangzhou City

Tasting tea below, Dragon ceilings of Red

Outside trees holding onto afternoon light

Sounds of Qin, Guzhen, and Erhu, Throwing me into a feudal past

China steel forged, Into Qing and Ming

Dreaming for your kiss, Upon the Moon reflections

On the sailing waters, Of West Lake

Viewing the great woman, Of the White Snake

Reaching for your hand, inside a high humidity bus

Feeling our new life beginning, From the Land of Dragons

The nights of joy, entering, Soft light flakes streaming

Upon scarlet ribbon curtains

**(1-1-2010)**

**Veracruz Mexico**

A Stranger

You are still a stranger

I was thinking about

How much I liked you

Being a Stranger

**(3-5-2010)**

**Cabo San Lucas Mexico**

I wrote your name in the Sky

However, the wind blew it away

I wrote your name in the sand

However, the waves washed it away

I wrote your name in my heart

Hoping that it stays

Nevertheless, the pain took it away

## (11-11-2010)

## Mestiso for Desert

When the wings of tomorrow

Bring us so much sorrow

I will take your hand

Kiss away your tears

Until the clear Andean winds

Brush away your fears

## (6-14-2012)

## "Faith Mind" by Hsin Hsin Ming

"Release it and things will be as they are;

Its essence is neither in going nor staying

If the mind makes no differences, all things are as they are.

In the end, ultimately things do not reside in ruts or rules.

No residing here or residing there;

One thing is exactly everything

Everything is exactly one thing"

## (6-20-2012)

## The Book of Five Rings by Miyamoto Musashi

"Emptiness is existence

Existence is emptiness

And attachment is the great heresy"

www.ingramcontent.com/pod-product-compliance
Lightning Source LLC
Chambersburg PA
CBHW071743020426
42331CB00008B/2146
* 9 7 8 0 6 1 5 6 5 0 4 8 7 *